THE ULTIMATE SALES SUCCESS

A List of the Ethical and Practical
Techniques of Top Salespeople.

Bernie Wimbush

BALBOA.PRESS
A DIVISION OF HAY HOUSE

Balboa Press books may be ordered through booksellers or by contacting:

Balboa Press
A Division of Hay House
1663 Liberty Drive
Bloomington, IN 47403
www.balboapress.com.au
AU TFN: 1 800 844 925 (Toll Free inside Australia)
AU Local: (02) 8310 7086 (+61 2 8310 7086 from outside Australia)

Print information available on the last page.

ISBN: 978-1-9822-9329-1 (sc)
ISBN: 978-1-9822-9330-7 (e)

Balboa Press rev. date: 12/15/2021

Contents

The Beginning

I was answering a call from a potential consulting client. He explained to me that he had made a great improvement in concrete mixers. He had found a way of making the bowl without any seam. He had made about 1000 of them. At a price of $500 each, he had half a million tied up in capital. He hadn't sold a single one. He explained that the price was only $100 more than the current price of his competitors. He wanted my help to sell these units wholesale. He told me that if you build a better mousetrap the world would beat the path to your door.

I couldn't take on the job. This guy didn't appreciate sales. He thought sales just happened miraculously but I could see the uphill battle to teach him about marketing and sales. I believe the liquidators sold them for hundred dollars each. Well below cost.

I had learnt the importance of sales much earlier. I also learned a very good salesman doesn't understand what he does. It has become so automatic and so simple to him that he thinks other salesman just need motivation. It is why good salesman don't usually make good sales managers.

My solution was to hire a salesman. So I did. It was great for about a month and then the sales dropped to zero. I didn't know what was going wrong, neither did the salesman. And that started this book.

I had to find what works in the real world. All the books that I had read, all the tapes I had listened to and all the workshops I went to, had great sounding ideas but they didn't work in the real world or for me.

We sat down together one weekend and tore over the presentation and the techniques which were being used. I was using my studies of the mind and how it worked to evaluate sales. After several hours we finally hit pay dirt. I won't tell you what it is, but it is in the book. It increased our sales by seven times. In my consulting I was able to increase sales of my clients by at least 30% without discounting prices.

Anyone familiar with sales knows we are using it all the time. In our relationships, at job interviews, in romance, in fact anywhere people are involved.

And you don't have two cart prices. Prices generally come out as number four in importance.

Definition of Selling

There is so much false information about sales, salespeople, what selling is, what salespeople do and so forth that it is important to really establish a useable definition of a salesperson and their product.

To define it, it is necessary to examine why there is a need for salespeople. Often people who are inexperienced in the area of sales think they make all their own buying decisions and this is simply because they are unaware of the subtle influences that selling such as advertising and peer pressure have on them. There are two main problems a person has, **(1) WHAT TO BUY, and (2) MAKING A COMMITTMENT.** It is in these areas that the potential buyer needs help. If you observe closely at the close of a sale, the buyer will go through all sorts of trauma. It is this problem that we are addressing, and anyone who disagrees needs to get some familiarity with the area of sales.

SELLING IS THE ART OF FINDING OUT WHAT THE PROSPECT REALLY WANTS, PRESENTING THAT TO

HIM OR HER AND ASSISTING THE PROSPECT IN MAKING AN IRREVOCABLE COMMITTMENT TO TAKE ACTION TO RECEIVE IT AND GIVE EXCHANGE FOR THAT PRODUCT OR SERVICE.

Too often people will associate selling with pressure, but if you look at the definition, you will see that if one uses pressure one hasn't got what the prospect really wants and so force is used to make the commitment. Anyone who has been involved in the training of salespeople will know that new enthusiastic and unsuccessful salespeople generate all of the complaints of high pressure. More experienced and successful salespeople have learnt to find out what the prospect really wants and so the pressure doesn't exist.

There is an element of honesty in the art of selling because the salesperson always knows more about the product than the prospect and so is in the position to find out what the prospect wants and give him a product that will not really satisfy that desire. The result is complaints if this is not done. Also, as we know there is a basic honesty that we all have and to deal dishonestly lowers self-esteem and results in eventual failure and/or leaving that industry. At best this gives short term success but the worst side is the destruction of the being's self-esteem.

One of the major reasons for the salesman's service is the difficulty almost all people have in making a decision. It is usually easier to do nothing than do something and so the salesperson's task is to bring the prospect's ability up to the point of being able to make a decision.

Let us look at a simple decision, to buy some petrol. Easy you say ? Look at the gauge, see it's under 1/4 and drive to my local garage.

Now just review that decision. How long did it take to arrive at 'below 1/4' as the criteria for filling up? Was it running out a few times? You see there is a wealth of experience in deciding when to buy and although it is automatic now, it wasn't at one time. Where to buy is another factor. Perhaps we have established a friendship or an account at a particular garage. Whatever it is the decision that has been decided over a period of time so that now it is automatic. The reason it is automatic is because it saves us having to continually make decisions. Governments often provide services for free in an effort to reduce the difficulty of the decision. However, price is only one of the factors and so even this method does not do away with the need for the salesperson's skill entirely.

Finding out what the prospect wants is probably the greatest skill in selling.

Obviously, knowing what the prospect wants assists in the decision-making process to a large extent. To have someone ask for a car is probably so far from where the want is to be useless. What is the purpose? What budget factors are involved? What models do you like or dislike? Are questions that spring readily to mind? The skill is finding what the person really wants, and so many factors will be part of the decision that to simply try to sell a car without really understanding the whole picture will result in a no sale.

Part of the salesperson's responsibility is the company he or she works for and his or her own finances. To not ensure the prospect makes a decision while with you means you have not handled all the problems and you have not really done your job properly and you and your company will not get paid.

Asking the prospect to decide is not a nice position to place the prospect in. It tends to remind him or her subconsciously of decisions from the past, not all of which were good. If you have done your job well you should know your prospect has decided and so it can be assumed. Taking this positive viewpoint will result in fewer traumas for your prospect and you will have done your job well.

Sales is an interesting profession, not the least part being the remuneration. The top incomes are earned by salespeople who do their jobs well and the lowest incomes are earned by salespeople who do their job poorly, typically they think of themselves rather than the service they provide. It is easy to tell a good salesperson from a poor one. The poor one doesn't make many sales. He doesn't make sales because he or she isn't following the definition above.

2

What Is A Salesperson?

There is such a lot of misconception about what salespeople do and their characteristics that it is important to tear these myths apart before new sales people start acquiring bad unworkable habits in an attempt to copy the stereotype.

When I've asked groups of people what they think are the characteristics of a salesman I get at least : *good talker, pushy, exaggerating (even lying), only interested in the money* and *insincere*. I then have asked these groups, "Who likes buying from people like this?" I have yet to find anyone who would buy from such a person, We have to conclude that this is not the profile of a successful salesperson. And in truth, this is the case. Unsuccessful sales people fit the stereotype and leave the industry.

A successful salesperson is a *good listener, truthful, mainly interested in the client's needs* and *very genuine.* There are many other characteristics but these ones are important.

In starting a sales career you need to look at the kind of person you would like to deal with and then become that kind of person. Customers are not stupid and usually have an ability to read through a facade, so the showmanship doesn't catch many

3

Importance of Attitude

An important factor in sales (or any area of endeavor for that matter) is attitude. When you ask someone to buy from you, an important factor in the customer's mind is who they are buying from. People judge on the perceived attitude.

If you present a cautious attitude when talking to prospects they will exhibit it back to you in the form of being more careful and so you will find them harder to sell. The idea is to have an attitude that does the reverse - i.e. a happy enthusiastic attitude. This type of attitude engenders enthusiasm in the client and it nullifies any unnatural caution.

One thing to avoid is a carnival type display of enthusiasm. The attitude of confidence, sincerity and strength is what should come across to the prospect. The prospect should see that you are enthusiastic about your job and the product and you will find that this carries you through a lot of problems before they have a chance to come up.

No doubt you can see the effect of a salesperson on yourself if you went to buy a product and were greeted with an attitude of apathy and an attitude of seriousness that made you, the customer, feel that you were imposing.

The word is ENTHUSIASM. Create it, act it and be it, keep grinning and life will go much better than you previously thought possible.

And sit helps to have an excellent product. Use your influence to ensure the product is excellent which helps you maintain your enthusiasm.

The positive mental attitude is part of this. Don't look at why it can't be done, keep your eye on the target and KNOW that it can be done even if you can't see how at the moment. KNOW that you can find a way and be willing to ask friends and colleagues etc for help but know you will win - despite all the "evidence" that says it can't be done.

Attitude is said to be 86% of the ingredients of success. As you get more experience it is easier to maintain a positive, enthusiastic and friendly attitude. Don't display poor attitudes to prospects or you'll find them harder to handle.

Keep Smiling and keep it light.

SALES TECHNIQUE

Building Rapport

Who do people like to buy from?

You should ask this question of yourself and I'm sure that you like to buy from people you like or are friends with. In fact, it is embarrassing if someone offers you a better deal than you can get from a friend. Many people seen to be prepared to pay a higher price to buy from a friend if only to support them. It also helps if you can talk to your friend if you need help later.

There are several intangible ideas that are part of this. Not the least is **TRUST**. A person we feel we can trust is a better person to buy from and so we are more confident that we will be looked after better.

The factor in this is **RAPPORT**. The more rapport the client feels with the sales person, the more he or she will be willing to trust and hence be more willing to buy.

Hence there is real importance in understanding what rapport is and how we build it.

NO RAPPORT = NO SALE

Rapport is defined as harmony or agreement. The components appear to be

1. Closeness or degree of liking. The more we like someone, the more we feel close to them. Some people just LIKE people and they find this is returned by others who in turn like them.

2. Agreement or common reality. We will have a better rapport with someone from the same club or school, even if we have never met them, because there is a common reality. Some books even suggest that sales people should falsify the agreement by mentioning something they are likely to agree with i.e. saying "I like your office". This misses the point that REALITY is more important and so when it is falsified (no matter how well hidden) it destroys the rapport. Truth is reality and you will find that telling the whole story is a powerful tool.

3. Free flowing communication. The better the communication works the better the rapport builds.

4. And all this leads to a better two way understanding

The first job in any sales situation, or indeed in any situation where it is necessary to handle people, is to get the communication going. The idea is to understand the other person and it is best done by getting the person to talk about his likes or interests etc. It must be done with genuine interest or it won't work.

Some people avoid small talk or asking about personal details, but people love talking about themselves and their interests and I've found that a good listener is valued highly.

Aim to understand prospects (or people you need to handle). Find out what makes them tick and how they think. You don't have to be nosey, just interested. Don't be so involved with your own interests and story that you must force it on them. Ask them to tell you their story and listen with an interested attitude. Try to get them talking.

The aim is to build an understanding or rapport and if you have been listening well, you will find out how you can best assist them with your product. They will <u>KNOW</u> you understand what they want and be more willing to deal with you. It makes people easier to handle.

5

Features & Benefits

To understand selling you must understand the way the buyer thinks. This can be difficult because he or she may not think about your product in the same way as you do. What you must do is put yourself in the customer's shoes.

Part of the job of the salesman is to fit the product to the client and this in part is what we call features and benefits. Your product (or service) has features. It may be red or with all wheel drive and expensive. (There are of course millions of others) These are features. But how will it benefit the customer ? So being red (feature) may benefit the customer by being distinctive and thus raising his status. All wheel drive (feature) may benefit the client by enabling him to go anywhere and being expensive (feature) may bgnefit the customer by raising his status.

Often sales people make the mistake of going into all the technical details when the customer isn't interested, instead of showing how these features will benefit the customer.

A way of saying this is that the customer has needs that he tries to satisfy and the sales person's job is to match the features of the product in terms of benefits to satisfy the needs of the customers.

Part of the product knowledge that a sales person must acquire is how the features of the product can be used to benefit the client.

This goes even further. In trying to make an appointment to see a prospect to sell a product, look at it from the prospect's viewpoint. What's in it for him. If the interview is not going to benefit him he will probably see it as "some salesman who is going to sell me something that will cost money which will make me short of cash to get the things I really want!" And you wonder why he says "NO!" or is even rude?

Why should a person even talk to you on the phone? What will your call have for him? If you can't answer that in a way that is a real benefit to him, why would he say yes?

Anyone you talk to listens to radio **WIIFM. WHATS IN IT FOR ME.** Talk to people with this in mind and things will improve.

6

Wants & Needs

Sales trainers often talk about the importance of satisfying people's needs with products. But it is not the total answer.

I have found that there are two aspects to people in this regard. NEEDS and more importantly WANTS. Needs are very obvious and logical: we need to eat so we need food. We need shelter and we need transport and so on. The problem is that it is all <u>BORING</u>. It's old hat. We have to have it and it costs money. Sell to a need and you will run into the problem of cost. They have to have it so they will chase the lowest price and they don't care about the quality. It's hard work.

Wants are different. They are the **magic** of life. Talk to a person about wants and their eyes light up and they show real interest and they don't care about the price. Oh sure they will talk about price (because getting a good deal is often a want), but it's not as interesting.

The difference between needs and wants is shown in cars. A beat- up old car is transport but a new Jaguar is MAGIC (it is for me anyway). If we bought on needs, none of the high price cars would sell.

Look at how Coca Cola advertises. It hits want, not need. The ads are exciting and "Magic" - there is simply no feature mentioned. It all hits at the wants identified with their buyers.

Finding wants is a skilled activity. You have to watch the person and see how he lights up. You may be trying to sell a savings program. To do that you should be starting with the result. Oh, it's to buy a yacht! and it's to sail the Pacific and that will give you a feeling of freedom. Watch the prospect come alive. Let him talk about the boat and the sapphire seas and the gentle Trade Winds and the sparkling sand. THERE'S A BENEFIT !! More than you could visualize - more than you could tell him. If he falters on the savings program you call him up and ask him about the sand and the sky again. That's WANT. Sell to it and you will find a new world. If you haven't got it, then the sale is a slog. And they cancel.

The Use of Questions

One of the objectives a salesperson has is to get the prospect convinced of his story. If he does this by a barrage of talking then the prospect simply "turns off" and stops listening. The prospect may even discount what is being said because he may consider that all salespeople exaggerate.

What must happen is the prospect must tell the salesperson. The truth is that the best salespeople are good listeners.   T h e y ask questions and they get their prospects to talk. In this way, they get to find out what their client really wants and also build an understanding of the way their prospect thinks. This builds rapport.

Getting a prospect to explain his objection helps him to see the error of his thinking if one exists. This needs to be done carefully so that the question is an attempt to understand rather than an attempt to prove the salesman's point.

To handle "I think it's too expensive" could be countered with "Why do you say that?" in an interested way searching for understanding. To have a negative undertone e.g. "Why do you say that (undertone : you stupid gink)?" will not produce any improved understanding of the objection.

Once you understand what is going on, then you know what is the right thing to say.

When I listen to sales presentations, I listen to hear who is doing most of the talking. If it is the prospect then I expect a sale. If the salesperson does most of the talking I expect no sale.

Use questions to understand your prospect and you will increase your sales.

SALES TECHNIQUE 7A

The first step to improving sales is to get a good understanding of the buying process so that we can understand what goes on in the buyer's mind. Having understood that, we can develop a sales procedure that parallels the way he thinks. Some of this will be unique to your product or service or company, but more of that later. In this issue I will cover, very broadly, some powerful principles that will improve your sales out of sight.

Who do we buy from?

There are lots of individual reasons and people will argue that it's the cheapest or the nearest store, but given all things being the same, we prefer to buy from people we know and trust. And that is the first Key. TRUST!

And how do we get people to trust us?

The first step is

MAKE FRIENDS WITH YOUR PROSPECT
What is a friend?
A FRIEND IS SOMEONE WE UNDERSTAND
OR HAVE RAPPORT WITH

To make a friend out of a prospect we must understand the component parts that build rapport or understanding.

I find understanding and rapport seem to be the same thing and understanding is a concept I find easier to work with. So I try to understand my prospect and I find that leads to trust.

We can break this down into three broad areas.

1. LIKING. It is emotional closeness. In fact, some people we develop an instant liking for. They show their emotional liking for others who immediately like them in return. They are usually a fun person and we are attracted to that. Its a skill and can be practiced. It is just being friendly.

2. AGREEMENT or TRUTH or SIMILARITY. This is the basis of many sales methods, *get the prospect to agree lots of times and you'll get the sale.* It goes deeper than that. The salesman who pays us an insincere compliment (something we might agree with) misses the factor of truth and hence loses the reality. In fact the salesperson who tells it like it is and is not afraid to handle the prospect who is talking

nonsense, will make more sales. We feel we can trust him. This is also about product knowledge. Someone who knows about the product he is selling and can make sense, builds this trust. Talking about it in a language we can understand is part of this.

3. COMMUNICATION. This is the key to handling people and to be good at sales you need to be an expert this skill. It has several forms such as VERBAL, PHYSICAL (i.e. handshake, pat on the back) or FLOW. By flow I mean the undertone that comes with it, i.e. the sincerity or otherwise or if its being recited from a script.

These three areas are all interdependent and add up to rapport. Insincerity violates agreement and so destroys the rapport.

Getting Offside with Communication

Next comes the problem with communication. If you talk <u>at</u> your prospect, he can defend himself by switching off and nodding at the right places. If you tell him something that he doesn't agree with, he will feel wrong and so will get even by not co-operating. He may disagree with you or simply not buy.

PEOPLE DON'T LIKE BEING TOLD

What we must do is switch it around so that the prospect does the talking and we do the listening. This has the effect of building rapport. You will have to answer his questions and also tell about your product or service, but what must happen is lots of questions that get the prospect to internalize what you're telling him.

Here are some words that can be used to turn a statement into a question and get the prospect involved.

Does that make sense? Do you agree?

What do you think about that? and so forth....

Acknowledgement

When you do a lot of listening you must let your prospect know you are listening. Comments, agreements or "I see" or "Uhuh" or similar keep you with him. Laughing with him also helps.In the same way, asking questions that show you are following the story keeps the communication alive..

Needs -v- Wants

People buy for one of two reasons: NEEDS or WANTS.

NEEDS are characterised by *HAVE TO HAVE* and are such things as food, shelter etc. If you sell to a need you will have to compete on price.

WANTS are what life is about. It's why we lust after a new Jaguar instead of a cheap old Kingswood. Get people talking about their wants and they come alive, become more animated and so forth. Sell to a want and your prospect will help you close the sale.

The magic of life.

So the fundamentals are, use *questions to build rapport and find the want and then give them that.*

Your Uniqueness

Every business has a uniqueness about it's product. Often the people in the business are so close that they have lost track of why people buy. It is vital to research out what it is about your product and company that makes people buy, and conversely, why those who are not your customers buy from the opposition. Identification of those factors is the first step to marketing.

Price

Price is usually fourth or fifth in surveys of why people buy, so don't get caught with prospects who talk price as No. 1. It's only a symptom of not selling to wants.

Asking for the Sale

Oh, and don't forget to ask for the business.

Conclusion

This document is designed as an overview of selling. The rest of the series goes into it in great depth. To become an expert, one needs to study and practice so your people can't tell you why it can't be sold.

Closing Questions

Having located the want and got the prospect to see how the product fits, it is a matter of asking a closing question. There are many varieties of this but the whole idea is to get a commitment. Basically the prospect must now make a decision.

> "Let's fill out the paperwork" or "What name will you want on the form?" as you start filling in the form.

> "Let's do it then".

"Do you want a red one or a white one?" leads the prospect into making a minor selection (of colour) and thus has notified his willingness to buy.

> "That will be $37.04 then".

> The idea is to confirm that the person is going to go ahead and buy. You want to finish off the sale. Or CLOSE the sale off.

Once you've asked a closing question simply stay silent and wait. Sometimes the silence is deafening and the temptation to talk is overwhelming, but realize it is the same for your prospect. Wait for his answer before you go forward. The idea of the closing question is to confirm that he wants to buy. Breaking the silence lets your prospect off. He can now go down this new thought track.

The order book close is where you start filling out the order form and then turn to the prospect and ask "Name?" or "Address?" This means the prospect has to stop you and once you've started, it will waste a form (which people seem to hate to do).

> Often the only reason a sale fails is that the sales person didn't ask for the order and so close the sale.

The most important instruction to remember if you want to be a good closer is, "Do you understand what a closing question is?" A Closing question is any question you ask, the answer to which confirms the fact that he has bought. The most critical instruction to remember when you ask a closing question is SHUT UP! If you shut up, only one of two things can happen. He is either going to go along with you or he gives you a reason for not going along with you. Remember the two most important words you will learn in closing are SHUT UP! The one who speaks first buys!

These following basic closes are going to require that you go through the process of learning them so that you can use them.

1. ORDER BOOK CLOSE (BASIC CLOSE)

This is the most fundamental of all closing devices. This is **number one** closing always used by every professional salesperson. You begin by asking your customer a question. Fill out the answer on your order blank, contract or agreement. For example, "what is your name?", "what is your correct mailing address or delivery address?" As long as the customer does not stop you, he has bought. Continue asking questions until you have completed the form. When you get to the bottom of the form, turn it around and give the customer a pen and ask him to okay it for you. Most people will okay an agreement but may not sign and agreement.

2. ALTERNATIVE CHOICES

The alternate of choice is of course the privilege of buying this way or that way. For example, "do you want your premium monthly or annually?", "do you prefer cash or charge?", what colour do you prefer?" The only word objected to is pay. You assume the person is going to pay. These are alternates of choice. All of them start out with the phrase, what or which do you prefer?

3. PUPPY DOG CLOSE

Do you know how you would try to sell a puppy dog? It's very simple. Just let someone have the puppy overnight. Many products are often sold this way. A person selling on this method may not have to close. The customer simply buys the product. The longer you leave it the easier it is to sell.

4. THE BALANCE SHEET

You may use this method on a prospect who is indecisive. You start out with a story.

For example, "As you know, we have long considered Benjamin Franklin one of our wisest men. Whenever Ben found himself in a situation as you are in today, he felt pretty much as you do about it. If it was the right thing to do he wanted to be sure and do it. If it was the wrong thing, he wanted to be sure and avoid it. This is how Ben solved the situation. He would take a sheet of plain white paper and would draw a line down the middle. On one side he wrote the word, "YES" and on the other side, he wrote the word "NO". Under the "YES" column he listed all the reasons favouring his decision. Under the "NO" column he wrote the reasons against it. When he had finished, he simply tallied the sheet and the decision was made for him."

Try this on your prospect and note the reasons why he should buy, but when he gets to the "NO" column, SHUT UP! Then have him total his sheet and the decision is made for him.

5. SUMMARY QUESTIONS

This method is to be used on the procrastinating client who won't give you a reason for not going along with you but just isn't going. We allow the client to say "no", but each time he says no, he is actually saying yes. For example, "just to clarify my thinking, what is it that isn't quite clear to you? Is it the integrity of (name your company here)?" "No", he will say. Then you start summarizing all of the presentation with one question at a time. Is it this or is it that?

Be sure to let money be your last question. Each time he says no, you have a yes, haven't you?

6. SIMILAR SITUATION

This is an old favourite of the sales industry. What you do is put them in another person's place so that they imagine it is them. We sell by telling them stories about someone and the person identifies with the characters and can make the decision. People will listen to stories - they like to hear them.

7. CALL BACK

There is no such thing as a good call back close. The only thing you can do to save a call back situation is when you go back to call on the person, you say "I am very sorry, but there is one important factor I forgot to mention last time I was here". Now tell him something new. Anything you can think of. Then briefly go back over some of the points you discussed last time. Now give him the entire presentation all over again. Be sure to add in the presentation, "oh, you remember this or you already know that." Then go into a normal closing sequence and don't even ask him if he has thought it over.

8. LOST CALL

This is the close to be used when you have lost it! This is to be used when everything you have tried has failed. Packing up material and then hesitate and say, "Pardon me, I wonder if you could help me for a moment." Here comes the switch. "Before I go, may I apologize to you for not being able to assist you."

"As you can see, I make my living by helping other people. Just so I don't make the same mistake again, would you mind telling me what I did that was wrong?" Then he will tell you what you didn't mention and you can say, "didn't I cover that?" Then your customer is back on the hook. Start telling him what you haven't told him about the product. Did you ever apologize for not making a sale? If there is a need for the product and you didn't make a sale, it is your fault and not the customer's fault. Therefore, you should apologize. However, when you use this apology you must be sincere. If you apologize with sincerity, you will find this lost sale close gets results.

9. MINOR DECISIONS

In this close, when the customer makes the minor decision, the major decision is carried. "As I see it, the only decision you have to make is, do you want to begin as a standard or deluxe? By the way, do you want to use your pen or mine?" There is an alternate of choice here but it isn't a simple alternate of choice. The salesman posed the major question but he didn't give the customer a chance to decide. He immediately followed with a minor decision.

10. CONFIRMATION CLOSE

When a customer asks if the program can do this or that, now is the time to sharp angle him. You pose the question, "Do you want it to do this or to do that?" When he agrees that he wants to do this or that, you have made the sale when you prove it. However, if you simply go ahead and prove that the programme can do it, you have no confirmation and no sale.

11. CLOSING ON A FINAL OBJECTION

Would you like to have a method of taking the first objection you hear, and having it be the last one? This is the formula for doing just that.

1. Hear your customer out.
   (Listen to his objection. Give him a chance to explain).

2. Sell him his objection. Expand it and look defeated.

3. Confirm the objection. Confirm it by getting him to agree this is the only thing standing between you and the sale.

4. Question it. Find out if this is the real objection and the only objection.

5. Handle it.

6. After you have handled the objection, confirm it by saying, "now that completely settles that, doesn't it? By the way, was that your correct mailing address?" and simply complete the order.

12. PROSPECT QUESTIONS

This closing opportunity is laid in your lap five to ten times a day. In this closing, salesmen have lost more sales because they have talked too much. For example, did you ever have anyone ask you this question on a sale? "Can I begin today?" The closing question demands that you ask "do you want to begin today?" If the customer answers "yes", he has bought. How many times a day do people ask you simple questions like these and you open your mouth and lose them, by saying "yes". If you do this when you have confirmed that this is what he wants, you will close more sales.

9

Handling Objections

When you are working with a client's want, you will find that the person will give you objections that are more like problems to be overcome and he will appreciate your help in overcoming them i.e. "I'd love to buy it but I haven't got the money right now."

The other objection type is a real stop. "I can't afford it!" even if you show him how, he will come up with another one. This tells you that you haven't got the <u>want.</u> Here you need to go back to why you thought he was buying and find out what he really wants. Get them talking about how it will be beneficial to them and LISTEN!

The first objection can be handled by using questions on the negative end of the statement i.e. ".... but I can't afford it." Here you use questions in order to understand what is going on that he can't afford it. Question it until you or he can see a solution. A more powerful approach is to ask about the positive statement i.e. "....I'd love to buy it...." Ask about that statement i.e. "When you say 'you'd love to buy it' what do you mean by that?" This strengthens their reasons for buying and uses the positive to overcome the negatives.

Taking it further you will find them selling you on the reasons why they should buy.

I dislike the method of coming up with smart answers to objections as it violates the "customer is always right" adage. Tell him he is wrong and he won't buy. Argue with him and he'll win the argument by not buying.

Make him right by getting him to explain his objection until he sees the fallacy in it. If you deal with <u>want</u> you will find he is much more co-operative and the sale is made much easier.

Learn to use questions to fully understand the objection and you will see them dissolve before your eyes.

10

The Salesperson's Objections

It has been said that in a sale there are two sales going on. The customer sells "NO" and the salesperson sells "YES". There is an element of this even when you sell to <u>want</u> and the customer is on your side.

What kills the sale is the objections that you believe are true.

"I can't buy advertising because the economy is bad." You agree that the economy is bad, and so you accept that that objection cannot be handled.

If you are always buying "the cheapest" you are sure to be caught on the customer who wants to shop your price around.

If you look at all your failed sales and look at what the objection was that you accepted then you have the key to more sales. What must be done is to study it and really handle your own objection.

Working with a colleague using the questioning technique until you fully understand how the objection doesn't make sense will give you a better chance of handling the sale.

Sales managers should work relentlessly on this until there are no acceptable objections and then watch the records being broken - if the salesperson won't be handled then s/he needs replacing.

SALES TECHNIQUE

I'll Think About It

Any salesperson worth his or her salt realizes that when the prospect says he "wants to think about it," left to his own devices, the prospect will decide "NO".

In my experience, so many salespeople have difficulty with this that if the pressure goes on to buy, most prospects can use "I'll think it over" as a way out of the close.

The first thing to do is to examine your own buying patterns. If you "think about it" then you will go into agreement with prospects that do this, and a small number will come back and buy which convinces you that it's alright to let them get away with it.

Once you realize that this objection can be based on lack of data and that when all the data is at hand people decide very rapidly.

Here's a handle :

Prospect "I'd like to think it over."

Salesperson "Certainly - what aspects would you like to think over."

This can lead you to the areas of concern and they can be sorted out as in a normal objection.

Here's another :

Salesperson "It's obviously not a clear "yes" or a clear "no" is it?"

Prospect "I guess not."

Salesperson "So what are the doubts you have?"

and handle with your presentation and questioning technique.

Here's another :

Prospect "Oh I always like to think it over."

Salesperson "Oh! (with interest) what do you feel that does?"

Prospect "I've made a few rash decisions in my time"

Salesperson "I guess we all have experienced (to build rapport) what happened to you?"

Let the prospect tell you all about it and then ..

Salesperson "So how would thinking about it have avoided that?"

Let the prospect tell you and keep questioning aspects until he can see how it isn't a good solution.

Finally, if he insists, ask him on a scale of one to ten how certain he is that he will go ahead. You may then be able to get him to convince you that he really is sold by asking why he thinks he would go ahead. You may be able to get him to start selling you on the product.

The further you can push this the more closes you will get. If the prospect gets upset, go back to the want and explain that you are only trying to help him see the pros and **cons.** When the prospect is upset at you, you've lost rapport so you must stop and rebuild it before you go forward.

So push this objection and learn to handle it.

12

The "Yes" Objection

Salespeople love to hear "YES" and hate to hear "NO". So much so that when a prospect fails to show up to complete paperwork not too many will call him to find out what's up and re-handle him.

The "YES" objection is the opposite. The prospect says "Yes I'll take it - I'll just go home and get the money" and the salesman waves him off - boasts to the sales manager about the easy sale and promptly spends the commission.

GOTCHA!!! the prospect had no intention of buying. You would have found that out if you'd offered to drive him home to get the money, but you wouldn't have done that because it might "upset him" and you'd lose the sale. Rubbish - you just didn't want to hear the "NO".

This objection is often used to get out of attending seminars, making appointments and similar minor sales.

The way to avoid it is to understand the prospect. Ask him to tell you why he wants to attend the seminar or what his interest is in making the appointment. If his answer doesn't make sense to you, i.e. there isn't an interest or want, you can bet he won't turn up.

13

The Hidden Objection

Often disguised as another objection, the hidden objection is hard to handle because you don't know what it is.

This means that the thrust of the handle is to discover what it is. There are plenty of objection handles to apply to it once you know what it is.

The most important tool you have is your rapport. Because he's not telling you something you've got a weakened rapport which makes it difficult (but _not_ impossible to handle).

So he gives you an objection like "I'll have to talk it over with my wife." You try to understand it, you question it to death and it goes nowhere. THAT IS YOUR CLUE. There is no change. Given that you are talking to the decision maker you can try "Apart from that, is there any reason not to go ahead?"

If an open question like that doesn't work only a leading question will. So if you've got some rapport you should have a feeling for what it is. So ask "Is it the repayments?" if that doesn't get it you will need to start at the <u>want</u> and go through the presentation step by step checking that he really agreed to it.

This is a tough one but it melts when you find it.

14

It's Happened Before

This objection has many forms but essentially it's the prospect who says - "I've bought insurance -(or whatever) before and got ripped off." Essentially he's had a previous bad experience and he's saying now is just like _then_.

The handle is to _use_ your rapport to ask him about it. Tell him you don't want to make that mistake. When he's finished telling you and he still seems uptight, ask him if there was an earlier time than that.

If not, ask him did he decide anything. He might say "All salespeople are crooks!" at which point ask him (politely!) how that makes sense.

If you do this well and don't ask your questions in such a way as to put him on the defensive, just be interested and it will work.

You could ask how this situation is similar, and then how it is different. Do this until there is a change of attitude or s/he clams up.

Having done that, you can present your product in such a way that he sees the difference.

This will work even if you were the salesperson he previously objected to but it's much harder because the rapport is harder to achieve.

15

Reading The Prospect's Mind

All good salespeople will have had the experience of knowing what the prospect is thinking. In fact, in my experience it is what makes the good salesperson.

As a skill, I haven't found it necessary to teach this, but what I have found interesting is the number of people who discount this intuitive feeling.

It is built from building a good rapport or understanding of the prospect. It's then that you get the feeling that he doesn't believe what you're saying (or whatever). As this point you say what you've observed. "I get the feeling you don't believe me?"

This is a pretty dangerous statement to make if you're wrong, but worse if you're right. So you say it. Even if he denies it, you will have defused it.

This goes for a lot of feelings you get from prospects. "I get the feeling you think I'm pressuring you?"

These are always stated as what you are experiencing otherwise there is room or an argument.

There are also the positive things. "I get the feeling you could really use that?" The fact that you make the statement in a questioning way allows the prospect to expand on it and thus defuse the negative or reinforce the positive.

Practice this a lot and you'll find it's uncanny in its effect.

16

BEING EFFECT

This technique is extremely valuable in that it allows your prospect to sell himself or handle his own objections.

In a spoken communication we have :

Talker -------------------------> Listener

CAUSE	EFFECT
RIGHT	WRONG
WIN	LOSE (in games)
ACTIVE	PASSIVE

If you look down the list under the speaker you will see the concepts on the left seem to go with the talker and those on the right with the listener to various degrees.

We all prefer to have the attributes of the left and hate to be effect, wrong, passive or to lose. If you take that view and concentrate on the left hand attributes (being cause, right, winning and active) then the poor prospect has only one way to show you he can win. He refuses to buy.

The aim of the salesperson is to make the prospect appear right, be the causative one and be the winner. To do this he needs to be effect and let the prospect be cause.

The use of questions allows the prospect to talk about what you want him to talk about.

If he disagrees with you, don't argue, you can only lose, let him explain what an idiot you are. This will defuse it and in next to no time he'll be back on your side.

I've seen this technique used when a company has said to its client: "Look, I need your help to price this for you. This is our cost and this is what we charge our usual clients - what would be the right mark-up to apply to you". You can imagine how helpful the client was and the margin increased over what the salesperson thought he'd have to go to.

Salesmen who appear to be fumbling getting the bonnet open until the customer says "Let me show you" is using the same technique.

This doesn't mean you appear like an idiot, but be willing to be effect and not so intent on showing your own power, and more of your prospects will feel safer buying from you, and will do so.

Answering Questions and Flying Blind

A salesman was once asked, "Do all the Jaguar Sovereigns have a sunroof?" "Oh yes" said the salesman "we wouldn't bring them over without one." The prospect refused to buy.

What the salesman didn't know was that his prospect HATED sunroofs. The salesman said the wrong thing.

This phenomenon occurs every now and then and a sale gets lost. The rule is don't answer the question until you know what the prospect is thinking.

Had our Jaguar salesman said "Do you want one with a sunroof?" he would have been told "no" and could have investigated what the problem was. He could have either handled the objection, or tied the prospect into buying one without a sunroof.

It's a point to beware of. Don't tear off at high speed if you don't know where your prospect wants to be taken.

18

Buying It Back

There is a point in a sale where the prospect makes up his or her mind to buy it. If you do anything at that point than give it to him or fill in the paperwork you run the risk of "buying it back".

The prospect has bought, any further talking, explaining or selling will only increase the opportunities to say something wrong and convince the prospect that he's doing the wrong thing.

Prospects can pick up your anxiety and that sets them worrying and so they decide to check it out more carefully or perhaps buy from someone else.

When the prospect gives you a buying signal like "Where do we go from here?" or "It will look good in the dining room" or the million different ways a prospect has of letting you know that he's convinced and wants to buy, sell it to him. Ask him to buy. Take out your order book. Go for it - it's yours!

Watch for the turn off, if you realize you've been overdoing it SAY THAT, say "I'm sorry have you already decided?" (or whatever you are picking up that the prospect is thinking), then give it to them.

19

Persistence

An important aspect in success in all areas of life and especially sales is persistence. How often have people given up just before they succeed?

I have seen that a major difference between successful salespeople and the unsuccessful occurs in the degree of persistence.

The ability to keep on making cold calls or the ability to keep handling objections is extremely powerful. If you are dealing with what the prospect really wants then you are not doing them a service if you quit before they buy.

You will feel uncomfortable as you persist, but this is your weak point. If the prospect gets upset, then you are not doing it right. You are not handling what is stopping the prospect from buying; you are simply forcing the prospect. You may have to reset the want or purpose of the presentation with the prospect so that you can proceed. Your skill in being able to find different ways to put your ideas across or handle the objections gives you more time. You may even have to come back and do a second presentation.

As you persist you will run into things like boredom and you will change some of your successful actions. Sometimes called the "greener on the other side of the fence" syndrome, it allows changes to be introduced that lower the success rate.

Don't miss the importance of tagging as a method of persistence. Set it up so that when you get stumped, you can call in someone else to do the sale or help with the objection that you cannot overcome. This is very powerful and enables you to persist even longer.

Even if you fail, you will learn more as you beat your head against the brick wall. When you analyse the sale later you will find things you learnt just by persisting.

20

Telling Stories

People love listening to a good story. It is important, therefore, for you to be able to illustrate points you are making by telling a story.

I like to use actual examples from real life - often about myself - to illustrate a point that I am making. Where the story is about someone I know, I change the names and circumstances so that the people can't be identified, but I try to keep it as factual as possible - it lends credibility to the story.

People relate to a story: they can see themselves in it and want to avoid the pitfalls or gain the advantages shown in the story. The closer the story fits their circumstances the better effect it will have.

Funnily enough, people don't tend to discount stories and this adds to the power of the effect.

Use stories and you'll find people easier to handle.

21

Getting Personal

If you think you can be successful in sales while remaining aloof from your prospects, you dream. Sales is a very personal activity and you are dealing with the things that make up a person's life, be it a house or a bow tie. The person's wants, desires and goals are part of the decision and you need to be willing to be part of it.

Most prospects buy or don't buy because of the salesperson. A very successful salesperson I know actually says to his clients, "I am one of the company's best salespeople and I'll personally make sure they treat you right. You see, I put so much business through them that they have to look after me and my clients or I would look for a company that would. In fact that's why I work for this company. Feel free to call me anytime if there's any, queries or you need help".

I've seen salespeople say to a client "The company has a competition on this month and if I can have your order today I can win" and of course depending on the rapport etc this approach is very powerful. People love to help.

I use examples from my own life and I tell clients about how we got the cat or when we got shipwrecked at Rotto as part of my presentation (if it fits).

Part of getting personal is the rapport it builds. This can work even for cold calls. A cold call approach I've heard goes "Excuse me, I wonder if you can help me? I'm testing out a new presentation and I'd like your comments on it." It worked not only because of the help flow, but also because it was such a personal approach.

Some companies insist on a script being used, but what I've found is that in cold canvassing or presentations these scripts don't work until they are "owned" by the salesperson. In other words the person learns to use them as their own. You've heard the phone canvasser who sounds as if they are reading a script. It's got to be natural and from the heart. You may need an outline to remember where your presentation is leading but it must come from the salesperson as if this was something s/he just thought of.

22

Sniops

The <u>S</u>ubtle <u>N</u>egative <u>I</u>nfluences of <u>O</u>ther <u>P</u>eople

This area has a major effect in all walks of life but it applies specifically in sales in two areas.

Often when people start in a sales career all the "well wishing" friends come in for the attack.

"Why don't you get a proper job?" "You'll never succeed"

"You usually fail at everything you try"

"You don't handle your own finances well, how can you be a financial planner?"

and so forth.

After a while, the SNIOPs can be

"You're always working evenings and weekends"

"You are your own boss, why don't you pick the kids up from school?"

"Why don't you ask your boss for a salary?"

and when you start to succeed and buy your new car/house whatever:

"Getting a bit above your station!"

"Now you'll forget about us little people"

The above examples are some of the not-so-subtle ones, but a raised eyebrow can infer these things and the negative pressure that this exerts can be quite destructive in a sales career. It is worth checking out how the spouse is going to feel about the choice of careers.

Now imagine what happens when you sell a prospect a product and he goes home all enthusiastic and raves to his friend, spouse or next door neighbor.

"You didn't buy one of those did you?"

"How much did you pay?"

"You were always a sucker for a sales pitch!"

"I know someone in the trade and he can tell you about it."

and you wonder why they call in the morning and cancel.

This is a factor you have to know when you make sales that are easily cancelled. The chance of running into a SNIOP can be high. Ask about it and get the prospect to identify the negative influences. You may need to resell.

Buyer's remorse is another phenomenon that people run into which must fall into this or a similar category. This is where the prospect comes out of the trance of the sale and goes "What have I done!!?" You can defuse this by asking about the second thoughts and the times it has happened before (when he made a wrong decision). Reinforcing the <u>want</u> and then reselling it, is the answer.

23

Inoculation

The old adage of "Whatever can go wrong, will go wrong!" is what we must handle here

If the buyer can run into "SNIOPS" or "buyer's remorse" the best way of handling it is to do it before it happens and not after.

One real estate salesperson says he gives each couple who buy a first home off him a packet of sweets. When they ask what they are for (or even if they don't) he tells them that it is for when they think it over and start wondering if they did the right thing. He tells them that most people do that and the sweets are for them to chew it over on. People often report back with interest the next morning that, that is what happened, but they don't cancel. He's inoculated them.

If it's possible that the spouse will object, it's better to ask what he thinks she will think about the deal, or better, have her there at the close. Get your prospect prepared for the SNIOPS by making him aware of what may happen.

Letting the prospect know that he may cool off will make him determined to prove to you that he won't and at worst will have him prepared for the eventuality. It is a variation of the 'Being Right' principle and gives you more control.

What you are doing is making him determined to prove to you that you are wrong and also strengthens his decision.

In the case above, as house buying is a very large decision, the inoculation works because new buyers may not have run into this phenomena so strongly before and when they are told that it is completely normal they don't worry about it as much

It's handling the objection before it happens and in this case it is the best defense.

24

Salesperson's Want

Probably more powerful than the prospects WANT is the salesperson's WANT. His demand for the sale and determination to get it are paramount to making sales. Without this s/he doesn't persist or use the relevant tools. He comes off the boil so to speak.

Nothing kills want as quickly as having his customers dissatisfied with the product or service. It's easy enough to blame the production department but this is only a cop out. He promised it, he better make sure he raises enough noise to ensure that his customers get looked after. The company also must understand the importance of satisfying the client's needs. If you use want to sell customers, realize that they are going to feel very betrayed if they don't get the full service or product.

Another area that kills salespeople's want is the internal negatives that can come in companies where administration staff give vibes to the salesman that he is overloading them or inconveniencing them with the paperwork. Even a sigh can indicate this. The result, over time, can be devastating. The salesperson is being fed negatives for good production and it is no wonder sales go down.

I've even seen a salesman who earned $250,000.00 per year in commissions sacked because he didn't do his paperwork right. The administration people got upset and rather than train him to do it right, sacked him.

Production departments can do this as well and salespeople can be negative too. The point is that the negatives destroy want and production goes down.

In rectifying this, one needs to start with the company's mission statement and start identifying all the negatives that are being used that reduce the WANT to achieve that goal.

Unethical techniques in sales (or any area) will knock out the want which is another reason for ethics in sales (or any area). Simply writing down a list of violations of ethics in an area will improve results remarkably -and even magically. Write them down with attention to details such as time, place, how and what exactly. Keep at it until your production improves. You will get some coincidental "lucky" breaks

25

SALES TECHNIQUE

Reverse Pscyhology

Reverse psychology is the name given to the phenomenon that occurs when something is taken away from someone and they want it all the more. Its our never ending quest for the unattainable. Its the instinct we have to do the opposite of what we are told.

Try to force your product on a prospect and he will back off at a million miles an hour. Tell him he doesn't qualify for it and he will threaten you with legal action if you don't let him buy it.

Watch for these phenomena in selling and you can use it to good advantage.

Say to a wavering prospect "I don't think you really want this" and don't be surprised if he argues with you and you just have to let him have it.

This is also about the competitive nature of people. If people think that someone they know has one, they are more likely to want it.

Sometimes a client is proving to be difficult and you feel that you are wasting your time. Don't just give up, tell him that you don't think he is serious about satisfying his want and see what happens. You have to be quite genuine about this and be quite willing to let him go. Sometimes they won't let you and will force you to sell it to

them. Then you don't have to take any of their nonsense.

<u>The Today Only Close</u>

The reverse psychology effect works brilliantly if your offer is for today only. It gets past the "I'll think about it" objection because its today only. Watch what happens when you have a house for sale and two buyers want it at once. Sometimes having only one for sale seems to draw buyers out of the woodwork when one person shows interest. This is the same phenomena. "If I can't have it, I want it."

So, making your product scarce, only for today or having some qualification can work in your favour, but watch that it doesn't scare off more than it attracts. Some people give up easily. In the face to face sale you can always back off if it's not working.

26

Handling References

The successful handling of references is a tricky area. If you have a strong client list then the use of them can support your cause and give you more credibility and therefore more sales.

If your referees are not sales people or don't know how to sell your product, beware. You have just put your sale in the hands of an amateur who very likely will say the wrong thing. A client who raves about you but puts a rider on it "Watch them though - they're good sales people!" is not what is needed for a timid buyer.

A list of testimonials can help, but if the prospect recognizes one it can be a case of the sale is out of your control.

One way is to question why they need the reference and handle that aspect.

Another is to get them to feel sympathy for the referee if he gets continual calls.

Perhaps another is to use the final objection close. "Is there any other reason then that would prevent you going ahead?" if the prospect says "No, there is no other reason" then fill out the order on the basis that the referee will say good things. That should flush out any hidden objections. I say "Oh he'll say good things - I wouldn't be silly enough to give you a referee who'll say bad things would I?"

Each product has its own peculiarities and so its important to work the area out. I always check with clients before I use them as references so that I know what they'll say and I hand their names out very carefully.

CONTROL = SALES

Keep control of your referees and they'll work for you.

27

Creating Want
The Demand Cycle

We know that in order to get someone to do something or buy something we need to get them to 'want' to do it or buy it. It is very frustrating when you can see just how much the prospect needs the product and yet at the end of the sale says "That's very nice, but I think I'll leave it." You just know that they did not get involved in the sale in the least and not only have you lost the sale but the prospect has been let down because you could have helped.

There is little point in telling the prospect, as he can still be detached and not involved. The answer is to get him or her fully involved. This is achieved with the use of questions. But this is about a very specific series of questions.

Here is the problem. Before you can go anywhere, he has to see the problem, then he must be able to see the consequences or effect of not solving the problem, then he needs to be able to feel the effect of the problem worsening. This is usually expressed as a fear. But it is an emotional response. At this point there should be an obvious need for the problem to be solved and if this is worked on it will become a demand and the prospect will be motivated to take action.

The steps go in order obviously and if you can't get to one step then the bet is that you haven't arrived at the step you think you are at. The prospect has been left behind.

Part of the skill in using this procedure is in keeping an interested attitude. If you try to push you will find that the person will feel unsafe and will bounce out of it.

STEP ONE:

Here the skill in asking questions come to the fore. You are looking for the problem. The thing that is messing up the prospects life. If you are selling cars, the unreliability of the trade-in may be the problem, if it is a house, maybe the old house is too small since the arrival of the baby. In our field, it is the problem that is messing up the person's life or business. It can appear as a problem, a want, or a pain. For instance, it could be a positive want to have more time with the family, or it could be the pain of an unsupportive business partner that he feels he cannot handle. It could be the problem that he is not strong enough to get his staff to do the things he knows should be done in order to achieve success. Keep probing until you can identify a strong enough problem that you can see will go where you want it to go. You will sometimes find it is helpful in checking to see if you have the real problem is to ask if he really sees it as a real problem.

STEP TWO:

Now ask about the consequences of not solving the problem. Questions that get the person to look at the effect of letting the problem continue. Again there will be an emotional connection. The effect of an overcrowded house, the consequences of an unreliable car or the constant pressure of the business when the staff won't do as they are instructed or the lack of time causing the hassles at home. Questions Eke "Are you willing to continue to experience that continuing?" or simply 'Do they want that?" or "Won't that limit your happiness?" And when they say "No!" you may have to ask 'Why won't it have that effect?" Sometimes it is necessary to ask them "Is that really the consequence?"

STEP THREE:

Now it is time to get him to confront the future. Nothing in this universe ever remans the same. It only gets better or it gets worse. He needs to confront the fact that this problem has gone on for some time and if he doesn't do something about it it will only get worse. At this point he will tell you that he will fix it himself. This means that you didn't get the right problem. The problem most likely is that he cannot do anything about it. If he could he would have fixed it by now!!! Get him to look at how much more unreliable it will get and how home will become intolerable or as the kids grow the pressure of the smaller house will become intolerable.

STEP FOUR:

By now he should be talking about the need to change. At the point he originates this, you can back off and get him to explain why it is necessary. Get him to convince you that it is really a need. Make sure that you are convinced that he believes that he needs to do something to change the situation.

STEP FIVE:

Now comes the acid test. Will he actually do what he says. This is the real test of the want. If there is not enough demand to improve the scene, it will not happen. It is a good idea to get him to see that if he doesn't make the commitment to change, it is going to continue as it has. This is done with questions. Often people do not recognise the effort required to make a change. It is like giving up smoking, as one wit put it. "It is easy, I've done it hundreds of times!"

There is an element here of recognizing how hard it is to change. The payments will be more. There is all the hassle of change and so forth. Putting it off by thinking about it is only giving the situation time to take charge and throw the person back into the mire yet again. Asking them how many times they have attempted to change or do something about the problem or the apparent problem might give them reality on what is needed. They need to commit now to have a chance at reversing the downhill slide.

This is when the signature goes on the contract or the steps are taken and the deposit or payment is made.

This is a powerful approach and works extremely well.

28

Sales & Control

In the process of making a sale, the more you can control the prospect the better chance you have of making the sale.

This is sometimes done by getting the prospect to make lots of little, minor agreements which lead up to the final agreement - the sale. It can be done by directing the prospects to sit where the salesperson wants them to sit. Another control method is the use of questions. This acts to control the prospect's thinking. Telling them doesn't control anything.

Even the Order Book close is a method of using control.

Some people think control is bad. If that is the case then they better stay clear of people, sales, management and relationships because there are elements of control in all these areas.

People actually like good positive control. What makes control acceptable is the degree of rapport or understanding that you have. The more rapport or understanding, the more control you can use. The more control you use the better life will go for you - in sales, the more sales you will make.

Don't be concerned about control. You decide what should happen and control your prospect into doing it. If you truly understand what your prospect wants, controlling them to get that will have their support as well.

So give them orders. Tell them where to sit and what to do. Control the sales area. Ask questions and get answers. If they get used to doing what you say they will buy when you tell them to.

Be strong in your dealings with people and they will appreciate it. And buy from you.

29

Uniqueness

Decisions are hard for prospects. In fact so difficult that governments devised a tender system to avoid the decision "The cheapest gets it!"

This may have worked well in yesteryear when it was a seller's market, but today there is nothing one can buy that someone can't cut some corners on and make a little cheaper. As one astronaut replied when asked how it felt to be on top of a rocket ready to go into space "How would you feel sitting on top of ten million parts each supplied by the lowest tenders?"

The point is, if there is no difference between the products then people will decide on price - they have to. However, there is no way that two products are the same. There is difference in service if not quality and there is the salesperson's interest in fulfilling the want.

In fact companies who are serious about quality control are finding it cheaper to buy components from one supplier to avoid the variations that come from 2 or 3 different suppliers.

What you must do with your product is discover its uniqueness and its niche in the market so that this can be used to avoid the pitfalls of selling on price.

When salespeople sell on price alone, they have just admitted they can't sell. They are simply order takers and need to be replaced.

Learn what your product (or your own) uniqueness is and make a feature of it, show the prospect how it benefits him and satisfies his want and pricing won't play a serious part in your selling.

30

Ethics & Selling

So many people have a misconception of sales and business that they believe you can only succeed by dishonesty and subterfuge. Unfortunately we hear of the occasional exception and think it is true. What we fail to see is that this is the way news sells and the vast majority of successful people are extremely ethical. In fact lack of ethics is a sure fire road to failure.

The factors mentioned in "Salespersons Want" are factors which make the dishonest person lose drive and fail.

In fact a survey of 1,500 people over 20 years showed only those people who had the clients interest at heart eventually succeeded. <u>NONE</u> of those who had <u>MONEY</u> as a driving force succeed in becoming rich.

Ethics can be defined as OPTIMUM CONDUCT TOWARDS LONG TERM SURVIVAL.

If a company sells to clients without a real concern for the client, eventually governments and press get involved and the company is wiped out.

False advertising is eventually caught up with and outlawed, and then the company has lost its successful promotion and so fails.

Customer complaints can really be destructive. Recognize a small number of people will complain about anything but even then it is a matter of making sure you weed them out. You can't give them what they want so why try?

A successful bank manager weeds out his difficult clients (who obviously go to his opposition) because he has learnt he can't satisfy them.

Don't use this as an excuse. Investigate the cause of complaint and handle accordingly.

Ethics is a very personal thing and can't be enforced by another. When it is, it becomes group morals and is junior to ethics. Only the individual can decide what is right for him or her, but this doesn't get you out of it. You have to observe what works. If you can't, then the group or society will impose its values on you and life becomes even more difficult.

The real test of ethics is "How well is life going for you?" The better it is the more ethical you are. If you want to improve life, improve your ethics. This can be done by isolating all the past violations and communicate them to a trusted confident. This results in a greatly increased zest for living and an attendant rise in productions.

31

Pricing

Pricing is a difficult area for a product or service unless there is a competitor who makes exactly the same product.

Your prospect sees price as related to value and that is a very intangible area. What value does he put on dealing with you as a salesperson, what is your uniqueness and what about the company? Let alone the product itself.

I have seen that often the price obtained is simply how much value you build into the product. The more it relates to want, the more value the prospect sees in it.

However, price may affect the volume sold. You might sell twice as many of a product at $20.00 as at $25.00 This has to be experimented with.

Always price is related to profitability so if the price at which the product sells easily is not profitable then a re-think of how to build value is needed. Sales skill is part of this and I have seen too many companies fail because they couldn't get enough volume at the right price. I always had a client in that same business who was making money hand over fist. It was always related to poor product or service or sales skill or a combination of all of them when they couldn't get price and volume. Poor service or substandard products can result in customer complaints and redos which add to the cost of doing business.

Sometimes companies reduce their list price in an effort to get business when what they should do is ask for the top price and negotiate down. This can be confusing to sales people, but the good salespeople often get the top price because they promise and ensure the better service. They also ask for the price and aren't easily persuaded to discount.

In the end there is trial and error. Keep a weekly profit and loss report and see what price has to be charged to succeed.

32

Record Keeping

Sales is a demanding profession. It is not for those who like to hide in a big corporation where one can escape accountability. In sales, results are obvious as are the lack of them. Very subtle differences can make a huge difference. So to succeed in sales you need every tool to assist you.

One such tool is RECORDS. In the rush of making appointments and closing sales and getting paperwork done it is easy to lose track of where the business is coming from and what works.

Keeping records can lead to better time effectiveness. One company I know investigated their records and found that 85% of their business came from referrals yet they spent 90% of their time on cold canvassing.

Another company found they were spending 50% of their time doing 3rd, 4th and 5th interviews on clients yet the records showed less than 5% of their business occurred after the 2nd interview.

Another important part of records is to see how you are going. Its easy to have a bad week and feel that you are a failure. I find it valuable to put things like interviews, appointments made, and $ value of sales onto graphs so I can see trends and not get caught either in the euphoric of a good week or the depression of a bad one. The trend shows whether you are improving or getting worse. This enables you to start taking action to correct or strengthen trends.

33

The Sales Sequence

A sale is not a single thing, but a series of steps that need to be taken to arrive at the prospect making a decision.

Each step consists of a particular state of mind of the prospect and a process by which it is converted to the next stage.

For instance the first step may start with a "name". The process that takes that name to a qualified prospect may be a phone call that checks to see if that person invests in real estate and can afford the negative gearing of your investment. Now you have "a qualified prospect". The next process converts it into an "appointment".

What you need to do is figure out all the sequences and each of the processes so you can build the "name" into a "sale". It is then a matter of perfecting the processes and the sales start flowing.

One of the errors that are then made is trying to take your prospect too many steps at once. If your next step is to sell the appointment, sell that, not the product. In other words, separate the processes. Don't use a process that is designed for face to face presentation while you are on the phone. Aim for the next step or it simply won't work.

34

A prospect is someone who you could try to sell your product or service to. In sales you should be continually looking for prospects so you can get a chance to try your persuasive powers.

If you don't know what your prospect looks like, how will you know when you see one? Often it is not how they dress or anything obvious, but an attitude.

This will take research into what are the characteristics of your current clients and what was it that they had that the ones who didn't buy, didn't have. Or maybe its what your clients didn't have that the others did.

The ability to pay is always a factor. However they may not have the ready cash but may have an ability to borrow. In that case the ability to pay may be based on the criteria needed to get finance.

If you sell new cars, there may be the factor of "sick of the old car." If that is the case then you may have places to look for them i.e. how long does it take to get "sick of the old one?" and then records of past buyers at that time span may be fruitful.

There is a factor about how serious the buyer is. And a simple test can be developed for this. New home salespeople get a lot of people through a display home, only a few are serious buyers and if that can be sorted out by a simple question then the strike rate improves. You spend less time on people who won't buy (they are not qualified).

Often you will find you have a list of prospects that have all shown a tantalizing expression of interest and you find yourself contacting them and answering queries and so forth. The problem is that you haven't realized that they are not qualified. You have taken "shown interest" as a qualification. It's not! So look over your list and throw out those who are not showing an <u>ability to decide and act</u>. This is an important qualification. By getting the qualification of your prospects right, you can concentrate on people who have a high likelihood of buying.

There is also the phenomena of "Who makes the decision?" Sell a product or service into a house and watch that you don't get "I'll have to check with the wife." The prospect is <u>both of </u>them because that's who makes the decision. One of the qualifications is "can he decide". If your sale is outside his area of authority he's not a qualified prospect. Find out who can make that decision - That's your prospect!!

On the other hand don't be so exclusive that you throw out a whole category of buyers.

Get it right and you will know where to look for your customer simply by asking yourself "Where would I find people with that attribute?"

35

Prospects – Where to Find Them

The first thing you need to do is to get **suspects.** Suspects are people who you think may turn into a prospect who you can then try your sales technique on.

Where do you find suspects? They are everywhere but what is important is the qualification of your prospect.

If you are selling furniture removals, your suspects are going to be people with or without homes. That's too wide. We can narrow it to anyone planning to move. But really, are single people who live in flats in a bad part of town going to qualify? So perhaps people who are selling a home are a source of leads to follow to see if there's a prospect at the end of the trail. So narrowing down the target is vital or you find you are wasting too much time in prospecting.

The next problem is a problem in making a mistake in the target area. For instance, if you use the yellow pages of the telephone directory you will be dealing with people in the same class of business, i.e. if you sell sales courses you may think that "car yards" are the area to attack. So you talk to lots of them and make appointments and really concentrate on the area only to find three weeks down the road that no sales are forthcoming. If car sales are down, then *every* suspect you talk to is short of money and so won't buy. Your sales sequence had a fault and the pipeline is dry. You are now short of money and it will take time to build it again. The problem could be that that class of prospect will all have an objection you don't know how to handle so you'll end up hungry. Vary your prospecting so you get a mix and you will be successful with some while you develop your technique.

36

Getting Referrals

A very powerful prospecting tool is referrals. A happy client will have friends or associates that are just like them. (Birds of a feather flock together.) If you can ask them who they know who could use your service you will get some well qualified prospects who will have a high profitability in buying from you.

The first problem you have in getting referrals is that if you ask for "people you know who could use our service/product" they will qualify their friends and associates and exclude some of them. They don't know what the qualifications are and will have a wrong idea and exclude some you would love to talk to.

The principle is that people they associate with are going to be like themselves. They will have similar tastes and interests etc. So all you need to get is "Who do you associate with?" If you can get their teledex and go through that you will have a list of prospects.

The first step then is to make sure your client is happy with your service or product. It's worth making a call on them and checking their perception of your product or service. It's important that you sort that out before you ask for referrals, because they will be likely to contact your client. Don't be "damned with faint praise". Sort out your client's perception of you before you move. If it's a complaint write down all the details. This really makes them feel you are taking it seriously. Then sort out the problems. Usually writing it down sorts it out. With repeat type clients just seeing ex-clients and writing down their complaints as they tell you and doing nothing else will get you more orders than you imagine.

Once your client is on your side and happy with you, you will find he is more than willing to help you. Don't be frightened to ask your clients for help. If you have a good rapport they will love to help you. People love to help much more than they like to be helped so do them a favour and let them help you by asking for referrals.

You can even get them at the earliest contact point i.e. the first interview before they buy.

37

Wasting Prospects

Beware of the phenomenon of the scarcity of prospects. Nothing is further from the truth. You need to get your prospecting up to the point that you don't mind losing or wasting a few.

This sometimes occurs with a bunch of prospects you are "working on". If they are not moving down your sales sequence you are better off tearing up their cards and throwing them in the bin. When sales are low and you are "working hard" watch that you haven't got a bunch of people as prospects that won't buy. Tear them up. Then you confront the harsh reality - you don't have any prospects. So now you do what you should have done weeks ago - go and find some new ones.

The idea is to generate more prospects than you know what to do with. Bring the volume up so you are comfortable wasting prospects - lose a few.

This technique is very powerful because it removes the scarcity one can feel. This has a very positive effect on your prospects. It raises confidence in you and so your product becomes scarcer and therefore more valuable and hence easier to sell.

38

Developing a Presentation

The fundamental that underlies a presentation is that if you use a gradient you can achieve anything. The idea is to take a prospect from knowing nothing about the product to owning one.

Each of the processes that lead up to the presentation will be designed using the principles in this document.

It is easy to underestimate what the prospect doesn't know and therefore miss educating him and so be surprised at the end when the prospect doesn't buy. With a good presentation you simply back track to where you left him and then bring him forward again.

Part of the presentation is knowing the sort of objections prospects have. This can be gleaned from looking over past attempts to sell and finding out what they gave you as a reason for not going ahead. This then is the basis for the presentation.

The first part is going to be a discussion about the prospect's wants. The next step will be going over the features of the product and getting the prospect to internalize how these features will benefit him in terms of his wants. The next steps will cover the common objections in such a way as to answer them before the prospect even thinks of them. You do not raise them but if he ever thought of them it is already handled.

For instance some years ago one tractor manufacturer found that a major problem in prospects' minds was the fear that the tractor would turn over i.e. if the rear wheels bogged, the front would lift and turn over on them and kill them. The motor cover was redesigned so that it looked like there was more weight forward and in the presentation of the vehicle was a phrase like "notice the modern look of the tractor?" It prevented the prospect from thinking about the objection.

Part of the presentation will be building value into the product. Asking about "can you see how the high quality stainless steel used gives longevity" is a building-value question. One presentation asked at the end of the building value section "so what would you guess this would cost?" the presentation was so good the prospect would give $20,000.00 as the answer when the product sold for little over $6,000.00

The procedure is to put down the objections and build a method of taking the prospect step by step through these to a closing question and perhaps a today-only offer.

Avoid using a set patter, but look at the targets you want to achieve and practise those using your own language.

Even when you have a presentation it is sometimes a good idea to look at the forthcoming presentations and brainstorm it in a group.

If you know your quarry and product you can come up with all manner of approaches which assist in getting the order.

Sometimes the strategy worked out does not apply when you get out there, but you have a better insight into the prospect's mind and the sale goes smoothly.

The other advantage is that it gets the group thinking about strategy and that improves presentations.

39

Problem Clients

Some salespeople try to sell everyone on their product and wonder why they are so busy handling complaints and problems etc. What they haven't understood is that there are customers or clients that simply cannot be satisfied. They have extreme "bad luck" and have lots of problems. I have written elsewhere in more detail about his phenomenon but what you are dealing with is a Problem Generator. They generate more problems than they solve.

The real trick about sales is to use your time effectively. The prospect who sounds like he wants to buy but needs six referees and to run it by his accountant and tells you how hes been ripped off before and gets you giving unusual guarantees etc for a $250.00 sale is worth sending to your opposition. While he's driving them crazy and got them running around in circles you can be handling the good leads they are now too busy to service.

Anyone who becomes successful in business realized that some customers should be sent to their opposition and they only keep the good ones. If you have clients who are on such a good discount and are such bad payers, and are always finding fault with your service (where your other clients are not) then you might be wise to review the terms of the arrangement and hopefully lose them.

Prospects can be like this. They make appointments they don't keep and keep asking for more facts and so forth that run you ragged. Go look for the easier to sell customers and see how many more of those you could handle. Start recording how much time you spend with a prospect and look at the optimum.

The whole idea is to get rid of the time wasters or tyre kickers and look for buyers. You won't have time if you have problem clients - you'll be too busy.

40

The Sales Manager's Role

Managing salespeople is different from managing production or administrative people. The fundamentals are the same but the emphasis is different. It is more important to raise the attitudes of salespeople than any other non-executive.

A common phrase used by some sales managers is, "It's a numbers game". Although there is a lot of truth to that statement, it promotes volume and not quality. When the quality drops the salesperson feels bad about what he is doing and makes all sorts of excuses for not doing the numbers, so the numbers go down and so do the sales.

The major emphasis of this issue will be on increasing quality (the relationship between contacts, demonstrations and closes), on behavior, and on making salespeople feel good about what they are doing so the numbers will go way up along with sales.

The major job the sales manager has is to raise the attitude of the salespeople after they have been on the job a while and have good product knowledge and sales skills. I say after they have been on the job a while because we have all seen the new salesperson with little or no product knowledge, no formal sales training and no recommended leads, produce like a top salesperson. This is a good example of the importance of attitude. I have seen experienced salespeople come to life and smash sales records (much better attitude) with some good sales managing, which I will cover below.

Selling

To cover the subject of managing sales I must first cover the subject we are attempting to manage - selling. One excellent source of sales knowledge is good books on the subject that really work well. There are many thousands of books written on the subject of sales. One book that has been recommended to me far more than any other and that is still in half the bookstores after being around for forty plus years, is "How I Raised Myself From Failure to Success in Selling", by Frank Bettger (Prentice-Hall, Inc.). He covers the basics well. Use this series and make sure people use the principles in there.

Don't allow negatives to come from any area about the sales team. Administration staff who complain to sales people about the inconvenience caused by all the orders created need replacing and at once. Use "Motivation through Discipline".

The sales manager should be setting and reviving games for his people. The games should not be internal ones of Salespeople against Production, etc. Sometimes a branch office going against another branch office works. The trouble with internal games is that they tear down the general team spirit of the whole company. I don't recommend any such games, even between branches. Publishing the statistics of each team member works well.

Games to break records for a day's or week's sales volume or for a month compared to that same month in previous years, and for individual records, etc., are good. Getting salespeople to publicly volunteer commitments to production levels helps them to stick to it. Once the game is set the sales manager must get the salespeople to keep it alive.

Games are powerful motivators but are often underestimated.

Praise salespeople who do well. Give verbal praise for well-done accomplishments. When they do really well, give them written awards on your letterhead or get preprinted awards for them from a stationery store. If they do incredible things, get them trophies, etc. Any bonus or practical gift to go with these awards should be token gifts only. In the game atmosphere people work mostly for the recognition and sense of achievement and not the money aspect.

A word of warning about goals : Some of my most successful clients concentrated on excellent customer service and excellent products. It seemed to them that one day they looked up and found they were rich and successful. The point is that yes, it is a good idea to set money quotas for the year, but to reach them you need to get your salespeople excited about the excellence of your service and products. If you stress money-money-money all the time, they will have a tendency to forget what produces the money and end up with less of it. Money is a gauge of the quality of your product and service and how well you ask for it.

Talk to your people in positive terms. For example, read motivational statements about "How it CAN be done" from books or articles. Get their responses to these statements.

Keeping your salespeople informed motivates them. In hard times, tell them what it will take to break even. Give them some specifics. This will get salespeople more motivated than ever to save the company, if it is done correctly.

From my experience, once one salesperson starts reading Frank's book, her enthusiasm sells other salespeople on reading the book. I would only bother reading highly recommended sales books as there are so many of them. This series covers all the principles I have seen in a lifetime of being involved in training salespeople.

Basic Fundamentals

Whatever you teach, make sure that you keep pointing out the basic fundamentals involved. Summarize before leaving a topic or subject, referring to the fundamental once again. You can help people only with fundamentals, not rote answers.

Sales Meetings

Sales meetings are very important, but only when they are done correctly. I have found that having three or four meetings a week of one to two hours in length works the best. The longer your meetings the less of them you would have. What to go over in these meetings will be covered below. Don't try to handle one-on-one problems with a salesperson for an extended time during a meeting. Other salespeople must sit around waiting if you do. Take the problems up with the salesperson after the meeting. The topics in a meeting must be common to all present.

Conditioning

Conditioning, as I'm using the word here, refers to a person having a bad experience with something and then making a negative decision about it for the future. For example, a salesperson making cold calls gets chewed out by a prospect, decides this is not effective, and makes no more cold calls in the future. This type of conditioning goes on with salespeople continually. New salespeople who know no fear, can produce as much as the experienced salesperson who has lots of contacts and referrals. As a sales manager it is your job to uncondition your sales people so they have both the experience and the positive outlook.

How do you uncondition salespeople? I believe the sales manager who did the best job of this specialized in unconditioning his salespeople. Their statistics went out the roof. He would have a meeting every afternoon at 5 p.m. and get his salespeople to talk out (discuss) their successes and sales barriers. The sales barriers would be the objections the prospects used to cause the salesperson to buy back his own product. The sales barriers were also those statements by the prospect and those situations that caused the salesperson to feel caught flat-footed, tongue-tied, uncomfortable, and so on. The prospects' saying "No" all day long didn't necessarily condition the salespeople. It was the barriers listed above that did.

This sales manager would also discuss sales techniques among the salespeople on how to overcome the objections that were coming up. The combined experience of all the salespeople in that setting was awesome.

Adding role-playing to this program, which I will cover later, really enhances results.

Unconditioning salespeople beyond this approach can be done using a one-on-one program. That program goes way beyond the scope of this issue.

Outside Negatives

The fundamental the sales manager is dealing with via his salespeople is what I call the "Outside Negative". The outside negative is the negative other people do to you that you can't control. The best way of dealing with outside negatives is not to try to get the whole world to stop being negative but to figure out good ways to respond to those negatives.

The one thing you can be sure of with outside negatives is that they repeat themselves again and again. So all you have to do is identify what they are and determine how to respond to them. In sales, the outside negative is usually an objection. ("Your product costs too much!") Your response is to bring them to a realization of what a good deal your offer is. Sometimes you have to experiment with different responses until you find one that really works.

It is mostly the outside negatives that condition salespeople. It becomes their own objection.

Motivating

This issue is all about motivating salespeople, but this section is to emphasize motivating them from the positive point of view. If your salespeople as a group are somewhat negative, these techniques won't work very well. Unconditioning and role-playing must be used to get rid of enough negativity that you can find some positives to work with. Long-range success in motivating salespeople is achieved by doing whatever has to be done to get them to keep themselves motivated.

Most positive motivating is done in a group setting. The ideal group meeting would be one where all the salespeople are creating enthusiasm for the group leader with the group leader doing these actions so the salespeople can and will create that enthusiasm. The group leader should be getting the salespeople to participate in the meeting. He should encourage them to volunteer questions, ideas, applause, cheering and standing ovations. If these things seem silly to you, just remember that they do work. In fact, this idea works incredibly well.

Emergency sales meetings work well to get your salespeople fired up when the numbers are dropping. You would start such meetings by outlining how bad the numbers are. Then ask them what can be done about it until you feel that it will be fixed.

Visualizing and affirmations are excellent, but this is not an area I have worked with enough to write about at this time. Napoleon Hill's book, "Think and Grow Rich", will be helpful in this area. It can be found in most bookstores.

Make up a credo of honesty and customer service actions for your line of work. Get your salespeople involved in improving the wording of the items in the credo. This does wonders for placing attention on what the credo should be. Remember to keep the credo alive after the wording is "perfected". Go through it again from time to time to get the wording even better.

Role-Playing

Get salespeople drilling doing the things that they do. Making appointment presentations etc.

Inspections

It is quite valuable to listen to what salespeople are saying to prospects and customers. For instance, if possible when cold-calling, have the salesperson record her side of the conversation. Listen to these tapes making notes to go over with the salesperson later. If you find yourself becoming upset by how bad the conversations are, realize that it is better that you know about it. You can also correct it.

Administration

Make sure your salespeople keep records. They should record the number of calls they make, demonstrations given, closes, gross profit, the dollar value of their sales, and any other relevant numbers. It is best to get agreement on this before a salesperson starts to work for you.

The purpose of this information is to help isolate exactly where things are going right or wrong. The sales manager should focus the salespeoples' attention on any imbalance. For example, a dropping number of calls being made when commissions are increasing indicates a future drop in commission.

Commissions

Salespeople on commission should have that commission weighted heavily on the profit from the sale. There should be charge-backs for deals that fall *through* or the commissions should only be paid after the customer pays and the salesperson's paperwork is completed.

Commissions work on volume when the product or service has a price set by management and where price is not negotiable.

A new salesperson can be guaranteed so much per hour they actually spend selling. After a few weeks they should go on commission.

Hiring Salespeople

Hiring salespeople is a vital area of sales management and is covered in the next issue.

Ethics

A sales manager should realize that one of the major areas that affect the attitudes of her salespeople is ethics. The sales manager should support and defend the ethical expectations of the company leader. She should work with her people to assist them to reach and maintain those levels.

Conclusion

The sales manager's job is a very creative one. Where I have seen it done well, with creative thought and dedication to the ideas I've outlined above, amazing things have happened.

41

Hiring Salespeople & Training

As sales is the beginning of the cycle for the production and hence profits and viability it is vital to have a strong team and to continually build that team.

Hire people who are assertive and have a strong ability to express ideas. Look for people who have strong beliefs in your product or service, and for those who want to be better sales people. Avoid those who just want money or who are easily upset by others.

A supportive attitude is just as important as competence. DON'T HIRE anyone who is weak in either support or competence. DO HIRE people who are moderately strong on both support and competence. Competence should be gauged on potential ability to be a good salesperson. Potential ability would be the right personality and the intelligence, not necessarily the experience.

Use the "Hiring Series" as a way of finding good people. I have found it better not to aim for experienced salespeople as if they are successful they will be happy in their job and caring well.

Someone with experience in the industry who wants to move up and comes up well on sales skills on the Wimbush Executive Aptitude Test is a good start. Use the Sales Test and interview thoroughly.

Be very selective in hiring salespeople and then put in the time training. Teach them everything in this series. Help them put together presentations. Watch for low conversation ratios i.e. high calls and low appointments. Don't let them fail. Work over how to succeed. It's in these issues so know them. Make them study at night.

Once they start getting successes you can ease off a bit but keep at it. The lifeblood of the company is in the sales team's hands.

If they don't catch on and don't start getting results don't be afraid to replace them. A poorly performing salesperson is doing something to your company image and to team morale that you are not aware of.

When you get rid of them the whole story starts to come out.

Sales are not difficult to make. Sure there is skill but the first seven documents of this series used well will get results. Make them use the techniques and get results.

42

Drilling & Role Playing

By role-playing I mean rehearsing. In my opinion, this is the most powerful technique available for making salespeople more effective. When you know the objections your prospects give your people and they rehearse with each other on handling them, you will be successful. The trick to the success is in how you do the rehearsing.

Before I discuss the rules of coaching and rehearsing, let me describe what a rehearsal should look like. One person acts as the coach/prospect and another acts as the salesperson/trainee. The coach controls the rehearsal by letting the trainee know the made-up situation, by telling him when to begin, and by telling him when to break or end off by saying, "Time out" or, "That's it". The trainee then attempts to sell the coach on his product or service. The coach must respond realistically. She should also keep the trainee rehearsing the same thing again and again, until she feels that the trainee has become so good that she can't say "no" anymore.

Rules For Rehearsing And Coaching

1. Coach with an objective in mind. Don't coach with the idea of being busy with the hope that something good will come out of it. State that objective aloud before beginning a series of rehearsals.

2. Coach one new thing at a time while continuing to coach the areas already covered. For example, you have gotten the trainee to say the words correctly but you can barely hear him. So now you rehearse it with attention on loudness while continuing to pick him up on any mistakes on the wording. You would keep rehearsing loudness, and the words, until he was good at that. Then you would add something new. You would continue until you were rehearsing everything.

3. You usually start with the wording and then, when the trainee is getting the words   right, you begin to work on the things that are not correct, beginning with the worst, then the second worst, and so on. Most of the "things" should be basic fundamentals such as "questioning', 'finding the prospect's want', etc. Do not- pick on things not directly related to selling, such as grammar errors and bad accents, etc.

4. The coach should have as many praises of her trainee as criticisms.

5. Rehearse each thing over and over_ and over again until you perfect it before going on to something else. A common

error in rehearsing is to be too superficial. The power of rehearsing comes from being thorough. Getting it right once is certainly not enough.

6. Rehearsal or the idea of doing it brings out negative emotions. These emotions are the barriers to quality selling. If you rehearse a presentation, an objection handling, or any sales fundamental enough, the emotion will fade away. The coach should be firm on getting the trainee to go through whatever they are role-playing "one more time". Trainees may try to 'discuss' things too much in an effort to avoid the rehearsing. Coaches should get them rehearsing while controlling discussions to an absolute minimum.

7. Coach realistically. Act like a real prospect would act. The best way is to remember and role-play prospects and people you have run into.

8. The coach, while being the prospect or client, should become increasingly more difficult until he is blatantly rude, sly, tricky, hostile, negative, resistive, critical, etc., but still sticking with the one thing being coached. This is done until the trainee is good at it despite the abuse. The purpose is to flush out any weakness so that it can be corrected. When a new aspect is added to the coaching the coach should go back to being somewhat easy to deal with and then increase the difficulty again.

    You can also ask the trainee what she is afraid of a prospect saying or what behaviour she is afraid the prospect might demonstrate and then do that as the coach until it doesn't affect the trainee anymore.

9. There are styles of coaching. You can let a trainee stumble through a whole presentation before giving a time-out with criticisms and priase. This is an easy way to coach. It forces the trainee through emotional barriers. Another way is to call for time-outs whenever the trainee goof. This method requires more skillbut is more effective when done well. The liability is that the trainee and the coach will get into long discussions and no rehearsing will occur. A third way is to use a mixture of both of these styles of coaching.

10. The coach's criticisms should be based mainly on what experts have said or written up on sales. Refer to the approriate book, tape or article while making the criticisms. You could actually read the book or article or play the tape. Or, if the expert is handy and willing, have her explain it.

11. Don't put the trainee on the defensive with your statements, tone of voice or behaviour.

12. The sales trainer or sales manager should supervise the coaches only, not the trainees. To do otherwise would be a skip of the chain of command. The trainee is the coach's responsibility while the supervisor takes responsibility for the coach's effectiveness. The supervisor should also use all of the above rules when dealing with the coach. For example, the supervisor would give the coach as much praise as criticism (Rule 4) on his coaching and the progress of his trainee.

43

Dissecting the Failed Sale

An excellent training tool is dissecting the failed sale.

Get the salesperson to tell you what they did or didn't do, what the prospect said or did and how it went.

If you have a good understanding of what a sale looks like or sounds like, you will find the violations much easier. Going over each failed sale in the salesperson's early days is vital to pick up the faults.

In this drill you take the attitude that every presentation should result in a sale. Check the qualifications of prospects and the objection handling. Sometimes you need to go on a presentation to find out what is being done wrong. Look for which principle is being violated and then re-teach that.

Sometimes you can get the salesperson to demonstrate what they do and that can be most revealing.

The aim of the procedure is to HELP the salesperson not make him or her feel like a failure. Find what is being done wrong and work out a solution for the future that will result in more sales.

The whole thing is motivating if done right and the sales build.

Tagging

This technique is taken from the Team Tag Wrestling and in that case it means you can bring on a fresh combatant when the opposition is at its weakest.

An extremely powerful way of increasing the closing rate is to have more than one salesperson at the sale. The way this is done is just when the sale appears to be over and the prospect is not buying and the salesperson has nothing further that he or she feels can be done, is to say "I'll just get the boss to drop in and meet you." The salesperson promptly leaves the room before the prospect can answer or object and gets the designated person. This person comes in and after the social niceties which build rapport, asks about the want, the objections, and so forth and very often can see a different way of handling the prospect.

If you set the rule that no-one leaves without buying or seeing a second salesperson, you get a higher closing rate. Partly for the reason that it puts a lot more pressure on the salesperson to close the sale in the first place.

The higher the status of the second tag the greater the effect in closing the deal. However, the principle works no matter who comes in to close the deal.

Use it - It <u>works!!!</u>

Cementing the Sale

At the close of a sale there is an amount of trauma the buyer runs into which is commonly referred to as "Insanity at the point of sale." Following that is the paperwork and the salesperson, having concluded his business is off and onto the next appointment.

Having built up rapport, its like losing a friend. What is needed is a confirmation that the buyer has done the right thing. A simple statement like "Well, I have to compliment you on your astuteness, you have bought our very finest model - I know you'll get more than you expected" is a statement that tends to confirm that the buyer has done the right thing.

There is a factor called "Buyer's Remorse" which is that feeling after one has bought something that maybe you shouldn't have. It is a good idea to make sure the client is still happy with his purchase or to reconfirm in HIS mind that he has done the right thing. Cement the sale and your clients will be happier with you.

46

Positioning

Part of a sales presentation is the attitude or position of strength that the sales person is coming from. This includes the first two preliminary sales - (1) selling yourself and (2) selling your company.

Selling the Company

Sometimes this is done by the size of the company or how long it has been in business or its corporate advertising campaign. Client lists can also have a similar effect. This can be hinted at by the salesperson to gain respect for the company.

Selling Yourself

Some individuals do it by having a grandiose title on their business card or by including the letters of their qualifications or memberships on their business cards. Using questions and building rapport is part of this as well.

The medical profession does this in an interesting way. Once graduated, a person becomes Dr Smith but after a lot of study he can become a specialist and becomes Mr Smith. It is the technique of understatement.

In the early days of Wimbush & Associates if a client asked "What's this Wimbush character worth?" We'd say "He's worth a few cents!" which was probably true but people assumed the understatement. It is quite powerful because people assume greater than reality.

Often successful people have a smaller than usual business card with no title on it.

Gaining position is often simply assuming it. When being introduced to a prospect for the first time a technique is to simply assume the friendship and greet as if he is an old friend (without saying it) and you'll find they start wondering where they met you.

If you want to be number one, simply assume it and handle customers and others as if you already are. In other words, assume the high ground.

SALES TECHNIQUE

Preparation & Planning

Just as in any activity, preparation and planning are essential in sales. There are several reasons for this and a number of different aspects to it.

Firstly, going over the format of the presentation and how you will apply it to your prospect will make you more familiar and confident - this will result in an smoother presentation.

Next, going over the situation in your own mind will make you more comfortable with it and thus enable you to think more clearly in the real situation. This will enhance the likelihood of success.

Going over the likely objections has an almost magical effect. You get the method of handling down pat and when you get into the situation you find it is no longer an objection. This can also be used when a presentation has not resulted in a close.

Go over what should have been done and then contact the prospect and go over the sale from the point it went off the rails. This has such a powerful effect that it has been referred to as selling by telepathy. So often when you contact the prospect s/he has thought it over and had decided to go ahead. Sometimes they call before you do

The Art of Telemarketing

Telemarketing or making cold calls with the telephone is an activity shunned by many, but it can be an efficient way of gaining new business.

People talk about fear of rejection but I have found that when it is being done effectively, cold calling is not a problem.

The major problem I have observed is that telemarketers usually put together a script and try to use that to make calls. It sounds artificial and ends up in a rejection. While you need an idea of where you are going it has to be real communication. Hence a script won't work. A friendly interest and genuine questions will get a positive response. The aim is to get a free flowing conversation going.

The next area of attention is attitude, often the telemarketer will get very serious and then the prospect does too.

KEEP IT LIGT!!

When it is a light breezy conversation it works very well. The moment seriousness comes in it fails.

To be effective you need to develop a real interest in people and their wants and keep it light.

The Emotional Objection

How often have you heard? "Well I pushed the prospect as far as I could without upsetting him". There seems to be a concept that you mustn't leave a prospect with a bad opinion of the company or some such thinking. Perhaps it is worrying about the referrals you'll lose if you upset a prospect. Personally I don't believe you get referrals from people who haven't bought your product.

What is happening is that the salesperson has run into a totally new type of objection the prospect uses to get out of the sale. THE EMOTIONAL OBJECTION.

This objection is not necessarily verbal you just get the feeling that the prospect will get angry or upset. The idea is to push on at this point *and* most times it won't happen. If it does you simply handle it and continue doing what you were doing. Note that you require a high level of rapport to do this.

The only time, you can get away with this is when you are following the want. If you are pushing *and* the prospect is not interested he will blow up because you are not with him.

So be persistent and don't be intimidated.

50

The Pregnant Pause

Although this technique is covered elsewhere in the series, this is such a powerful technique that it is vital to examine it in isolation.

The basic is that most people cannot tolerate a silence when faced by another person. If you ask a question and simply wait, the other person will start talking.

If you ask a closing question, such as "Do you want a red one or a green one?" and then simply wait, looking at the person, you will create enormous pressure and the prospect will feel compelled to answer. Don't take that pressure off by breaking the silence.

When used in negotiation, this technique is covered by the phrase "He who speaks first, loses".

You can even open conversations by silence. Look expectant and the other person will start talking.

If the person you are negotiating with knows the technique he will be aware of what you are doing but it still works.

Nodding slightly can initiate and/or elicit agreement from the person. It also takes some of the potential or perceived hostility off an immobile *pregnant* pause because they think you're with them. So if the consultant/salesperson asks a "Yes or No" question such as "Can   you see the value of ...?", the purchaser perceives the nodding as an agreement and will be more easily encouraged into saying "Yes". This is related to the acknowledgement so essential in communication but encourages the person talking to continue. This in turn gives you valuable data about your prospect.

51

A Cause

The drive of a sales team is dependent on the want the salespeople have for the product to be in the hands of the public. Although want is always an important factor in successful selling, want as a cause has further application in realising a company's goals.

An excellent mission statement can become a cause and when this happens the team becomes incredibly devoted to the group and it's production. (It not only applies to sales but to all parts of an organization).

We see this in the religious fanatic, the ardent unionist, the political activist and a host of others. It is simply the nature of the game. It is believed to be so important that the individual pales into insignificance. Often the leaders of such groups see the power without understanding the whole picture of people and take advantage of the group. This leads to destruction of the group and the individuals of course. It looks crazy, and so it is, but there are causes that are not crazy, so there is no reason not to use this power.

The idea is to develop the mission statement of the group to a point where it is an all-consuming goal. This then gives the group a better chance of growth and hence the individuals grow as do the public that receive the product or service.

The use of a cause is a powerful tool and should not be overlooked in the development of a sales team or in any team for that matter.

52

Telling Them

I've written so much about the questioning technique that it would be possible to get the view that a salesperson shouldn't talk or tell a prospect anything. This is not so.

In sales CONTROL =INCOME

What is control - it is getting the other person to do what you want. The amount of control you <u>can </u>use is dependent on RAPPORT so

RAPPORT = CONTROL = INCOME

When it comes time to tell a prospect something you must come from a position of strength. its more how you tell them than what you tell them (though that is important).

So you tell them facts without a hint of doubt or reservation in your voice. You are very certain yourself and you state it that way. There is an element of truth in this as the lie always seems to wreck the power. But again some seem to be very convincing in their lies. What I have noticed is they seem to catch the people who are victims anyway. And that makes sense to me, unethical people (victims) relate best to unethical people and have rapport with them.

Being apologetic or timidly putting forward a proposition doesn't work. Be sure of your ground and give it to them at full force.

SIMPLE

DIRECT

STRONG

These are the words that best describe the delivery that gets across.

Listen to good salespeople, or good speakers and you will hear this unreserved power. It may be quiet, but you know the speaker knows it and puts it across without reservation.

Simply take the high ground by assuming it and speak with authority and truth and watch the results.

When people speak of "Presence" it is these things they are noticing. This "Confidence" and power. Its wrapped around a good understanding of the audience and a real certainty about what is being said and an enthusiastic attitude.

But don't forget questions

53

Prospects – How to Get Them

Prospecting is a vital aspect of sales but can be a long grinding slog that results in low morale.

One cause of this is unrealistic expectations. If a sales person sets a target of 10 prospects per day and can't do this, or doesn't do this, then he will feel badly about his production. This makes him less motivated so the calls don't go well and he gets less results and must spend more time working at it. This results in failure.

What I found was, by setting the target of one appointment per day, (a target that suited our particular business production), the team became more motivated. The idea was that the salesperson was to work on prospecting until one appointment was made. This done, the idea was to get on to more fun activities like seeing old clients or consulting etc. This did two things:

- No longer were salespeople putting in hours "prospecting". They were result orientated. They did it until one appointment was made. The sooner the better.

- Secondly, it was easy to monitor. Around 12 noon, I could ask people if they had made their appointment. If not we could work out what was wrong and fix it.

The overall result was more appointments than ever before. So find the part of the sale that's hard to do and get it done in small comfortable targets.

54

The Ethnic Discount

In some cultures bargaining is a way of life and when you are dealing with them there is a potential problem that must be allowed for.

When you state your price some people will immediately believe that the price can be negotiated down. Hence you receive an offer. However, if you haven't left room to negotiate you are in an awkward position. When you say "no discounts" you are telling the prospect that they are wrong and this can lose the sale.

One solution is to state a price higher than you expect, and then allow yourself to be negotiated down. This has the advantage of you getting your price and the prospect winning by getting you down.

My tip is to use it as a "today only" offer. That is, only accept the lower offer if its a genuine offer and they sign up today. It can also be done by having your contract set up as an offer and get them to put the offer in writing and then someone else can accept it, making it binding.

55

Buyers Remorse

In selling anything you can get the prospect to the point of agreement and then have the client swing up later and cancel. The buyer has "thought it over" and changed his mind. This is termed "Buyers Remorse".

The solution for this is to inoculate against it. One real estate salesman gives his clients a packet of M + M's when he signs them up. When they ask "Why?" he tells them that everyone gets home and thinks "What have I done?" and gets scared. He explains this is normal and is something most people go through. He reports that often his clients ring the next day and tell him that that is exactly what happened. But they don't cancel.

With every product there is a buyers remorse and it requires different inoculation.

With self-improvement we are pushing people through a sub-conscious comfort-zone and life and people will act to pull them back in the mire. This is even more so with wives, husbands, partners, bosses, P.G.'s and so forth. These people get worried that the client will change and may not be so easy to manipulate or be so comfortable. Hence they may bring pressure to bear to stop the person. A different form of buyers remorse.

The solution is to inoculate. Get a solid commitment. Real winners understand this and push through. They decide quickly and stick with it. Losers decide slowly and change their minds at the slightest discomfort. So inoculate and handle it.

56

Putting Up Prices

How often do we get a flyer in the mail from our regular supplier advising that prices have gone up yet again?

The problem with this is that it is a written communication which can upset, and worse get us focused on the price. And there are always competitors out there willing to supply at a lower price. In fact this is a poor technique that I have seen. Get the customer on board by offering low prices and then send round this flyer.

This is simply dumb.

Sales is about getting rapport with a client to establish his want, making your product and service real to him to achieving his want and the value of this is such that he is willing to pay your price. The repeat sale requires the continued rapport and the re-establishment that your product and service is assisting him to achieve his want. He will *continue* to buy and the price is no longer a major factor.

You need to be in regular communication with customers and if prices are going to go up, this is a new sale and should be handled by a salesperson, not a letter.

Don't take customers for granted. Your opposition is looking for a way to take them off you and if you handle them well, you should be in a position to smooth over the increase much easier than the competition can get the rapport etc to take them away.

Emotion in Selling

It has long been said that people buy on emotion and then justify it on logic. The most staid accountants and engineers will deny this but that is still the way they buy.

So the selling presentation must get the prospect emotional about the purchase. This is why NEED is such a poor selling tool. It is too logical.

WANT (or avoidance of pain) is an emotional issue and so is a powerful tool to get the prospect to buy. Get into the problem solving side and the emotion of that before you get into technical details.

Don't be afraid to enter your own emotion into a sale because it will assist the client in the buying process.

58

Selling the Sizzle

When people say "Sell the Sizzle, not the Steak" what are they telling us?

It is not the product that the customer wants. It is the romance or want that surrounds it.

I know a Jaguar salesman who used to get a customer in the car and then race it round a stretch of curved road along the river and then park it on the green grass of the Yacht Club and wander across the road with his prospect, to look at the picture the car made with the water, the lawn and the boats in the background. That's sizzle!

A technique I use once I have found just how someone wants to improve is to tell them that I'd love to help them achieve that. I have a genuine interest and desire to make it happen and clients find this is a real benefit to have someone so interested to make it all happen.

Sizzle is the benefit one gets from the product. Not the product itself.

So put yourself by the BBQ and listen to that steak sizzling away with the aroma attacking you tastebuds ... no wonder some people prefer it rare. Who can wait?

59

Dissecting Successes

In Sales Series I have talked about dissecting the failed sale, but there is a wealth of importance to be gained from the dissecting of a success.

New ideas have a 97% chance of not working or failing so if you can find what has worked in the past and then concentrate on that you will become more successful faster.

So when it works, take it apart and find what you did that worked. When you find it, write it down and put it in a file marked, "SUCCESSFUL ACTIONS".

Beware of ideas that really are out of this world, but look for things that are repeatable and which follow the basic principles. I listen to old people who are asked for the secret to their longevity and they often come up with things that simply don't make sense.

In sales however, to find what works and write it down is fantastic when you hit a slum and read the file. It will revitalize you.

Just reading the Successful actions file every few months can be quite enlightening.

Calling the Moment

This is the technique of asking or stating what you observe <u>when you observe it.</u>

For instance the prospect you are talking to is being very cautious and you get the feeling he is worried about being sold something - so you say "Are you worried I might sell you something?" He may deny this, but if you are right he will change and be more malleable.

This has many variations and is used in a way that doesn't make the prospect feel wrong. For instance, "I get the feeling you don't believe me." As a statement this is non-accusative and he can't really argue that you don't get the feeling. This may be followed by, "Why do you think I might feel that way?"

It is very confrontive, but very effective and it needs to be practised. Say what you observe and see what happens.

It works because it hits at the truth and when the person confronts it he can no longer hold it as true and it goes.

61

Giving Customers to
the Opposition

In sales there is a factor of qualification. This is sometimes seen as having the ability and intent to buy a product. There is more to it than that.

The customer is your employer in a way. He supplies the money to keep the business going. If he is too small he may not buy enough product to keep you going.

Often there is a hidden cost in a business - the cost of getting a customer. If a rep spends a lot of time getting a very small customer, there may not be enough profit in the resulting business to pay the rep. If he continues to get business like that the company will incur a loss because of the cost of getting that unprofitable business. Comments like "Every little bit helps" hide the fact that the rep should be chasing bigger clients.

You can divide the overheads and salaries associated with each rep by the number of visits he makes. This is then the cost of a call. When you've done that, you will see how much each call must generate.

The next Qualification is how difficult the customer is to deal with. He may push for unrealistic discounts so you can't afford to give him the service or he may just give you so many hassles that you or your staff keep making mistakes so he can put you under more pressure. He may pay late or only pay after hassle him.

So go through your customer lists and eliminate those customers that are unprofitable, ie bad payers, high discounts, low volume, difficult customers and get rid of them or handle them to fit your business so it is worth handling them.

The result is that you will have more time to look for profitable business while your troublesome clients go to your opposition and destroy his business.

62

The Factory Tour

One of the most fascinating sales techniques is getting a tour of the factory. The guy in charge is usually very proud of what he has built up and only rarely gets to show it off.

So, be interested enough and ask for a tour. Ask questions and let him talk. Don't pretend to be interested - be interested. Listen to his story. Find out how he got to where he is. Acknowledge his hard work, skill, etc etc.....

This technique is extremely powerful in building rapport. Use it and improve your relationship with your client.

The On Sale

The hardest sale to make is the first sale. Once you have sold the client has demonstrated confidence in you and now becomes your best source of prospect.

The problem is that now you have satisfied the "want". But have you?

This is where good salespeople make sales. They develop rapport, then trust, and so understand the customer.

What accessories can you sell so he can use the product. Will he buy another of your associated products?

Can you get a referral? This may be how you sell another product. Get him to recommend you to another client.

Existing customers are your best source of the best business. REPEAT BUSINESS.

The first sale is the most expensive. From there it is much more profitable. In fact the "loss leader" is a technique to get customers into the shop to buy something, so you can sell something else, ie bread sold at 47c which costs $1.50 is used as a "loss leader" to get people into the store to buy $100 of groceries at reasonable margins. You can do this too!

64

The Cold Call

When making cold calls it is important to focus on the customer. If you are interrupting them then there has to be a perceived value for them in listening to your story.

Hence there is importance in first impressions and benefits.

For instance if we use `We work one to one with business leaders." we get an immediate hang up. He doesn't care what we do. He wants to know what we can do for him that is important to him.

If we use "We have a unique system of building synergy among your employees." we get greater interest. We then follow with "...for instance we deal with employees who don't work up to your standards, who come to work alright but seem to lack the motivation to go the extra mile .... YOU HAVE SEEN THAT, RIGHT?" (not `have you seen that?' which is usually met with a no.)

Now we can say "......that is what we specialise in......" and simply close on the appointment.

Strong statements which are on the prospects interest with questions that lead town appointment.

More On Want

Want is the most powerful too in the art of handling people. If you can find out what people want then there is usually little difficulty in finding how to satisfy that want and thus creating a "win-win" situation.

Want however comes in three disguises and it is important to understand each one so that you can utilize them all and thus increase you expertise in the area.

Want can appear as 'PAIN', 'PROBLEM' or just plain 'WANT'.

PAIN: This is where the situation is so unbearable that the person wants immediate and total relief and they want it NOW!!! This is the most obvious and so many businesses only cater to this area. However even in this one there can be other more subtle wants and many the liquidator has been called into a company to solve the PAIN of pressing creditors to miss out on the job of winding up the company because a more subtle WANT was not found.

PROBLEM: Some people try to avoid this word and replace it with 'challenge' but when someone has a pressing problem there is usually so much want to get rid of it that it that it becomes an all important focus and the person who can solve it for them gets a great deal of credibility.

WANT: This is often expressed as 'what is important'. However, many people have had their wants so suppressed, that they hid what they really want and give what is expected. Probe around and no matter how suppressed it is or how illogical it appears to the person it will rehabilitate the life in the person and you will have their undivided attention, they will become more animated and they will be motivated again.

So study the people you wish to handle or motivate or sell to and you will find their 'hot button' appears in one of the three forms above and if you work with it you will find you can hold their attention. If you then go further and actually deliver what you promise or even more then the world becomes your oyster as the saying goes.

Recruiting – A Two Way Sales Process

Often in going through the challenges of finding someone who is thought to be the best fit in the recruiting process, the other side is neglected.

Just as the candidate is trying to sell you on 'buying' him or her, there is another sale going on. This is the sale of the position to the candidate.

Going through the rigorous testing process of course makes the approach feel more professional and it makes it more scarce and much more of a challenge. These things automatically build want. But does the candidate understand how it fits his basic want?

The basic rules of selling must be applied at the point you decide to appoint. At this point the artificial things like challenge and scarcity go. You must find his want and make sure that he understands how your company will meet those wants. What problems were in his last position and how does you company handle that.

Remember that for the first few weeks he will not feel secure in the new environment and the work done at appointment can make the difference between keeping a good employee and having to do it all over again.

www.ingramcontent.com/pod-product-compliance
Lightning Source LLC
Chambersburg PA
CBHW072046230526
45468CB00019B/318

* 9 7 8 1 9 8 2 2 9 3 2 9 1 *